Published By Adam Gilbin

@ Cody Smith

Fat Loss: a Step-by-step Guide to the Secret of

Healthy Recipes for Weight Loss Without Dieting

All Right RESERVED

ISBN 978-87-94477-75-8

TABLE OF CONTENTS

Lasagna Zucchini Cups 1

Beef Zucchini Enchiladas 4

Keto Zucchini Taco Shells 7

Chocolate Cherry Smoothie 10

. Antioxidant Wake Up Smoothie 11

Crunchy Nut Coleslaw 12

Maple Syrup 14

Taco Salad 15

Red Curry 16

Hearty Avocado Salad 18

Spiced Tuna Salad 20

Flax And Blueberry Vanilla Overnight Oats 22

Savory Chowder 24

Greek Yogurt With Mixed Berries, Honey, And Granola 26

Salad With Mixed Greens, Tomatoes, Cucumbers, Olives, Feta Cheese, And Lemonolive Oil Dressing 28

Grilled Salmon With Lemon And Dill, Served With
Roasted Asparagus And Quinoa 29

Hummus With Carrot Sticks 31

Green Detox Elixir With Lemon And Ginger 34

Fat Burning Cocktail With Grapefruit And Orange 36

Smoothie Bowl 38

Mushroom Baked Eggs With Squished Tomatoes 40

Apple & Sultana Porridge 42

Cardamom & Peach Quinoa Porridge 43

Forest Fruit & Banana Smoothie 45

Creamy Yogurt Porridge 46

Garlic & Bay Tilapia 47

Strawberry & Banana Smoothie 49

Garlic & Kale Soup 50

Red Wine Chicken 51

Shish Kebab With Lemon Tahini Sauce 54

Barbecue Chicken Pizzas 55

Tomato Herb Marinated Flank Steak 57

- Roasted Pork Tenderloin With Rhubarb Bbq Sauce 59
- Seared Salmon With Sugar Snap Fennel Slaw 62
- Mussels With Italian Turkey Sausage, Tomato & Basil ... 65
- Bang Cauliflower 67
- Butternut Squash Noodles 70
- Burrito Butternut Squash Boats 71
- Quinoa Salad From The Mediterranean 75
- Broccoli And Almond Salad With Alkalinity 77
- Avocado And Cucumber Salad 79
- Stuffed Bell Peppers 80
- Zucchini Noodles With Pesto 82
- Roasted Cauliflower Bowl 84
- Mexican Tortilla Soup 86
- Lemon Chicken Stir Fry 88
- Eggs With Ham, Cheddar And Chives 90
- Veggie Smoothie 92
- Blueberry, Flaxseed Yogurt 93
- Salmon Fillet With Citrus & Thyme 94

- Kale, Edam Me And Tofu Curry 96
- Salmon Sirt Super Saladsirt Food 99
- Turkey Skinny Stay Skewers 101
- Broiled Ginger Lime Chicken 104
- Sirtfood Bites 106
- Lima Bean Dip 108
- Apple And Leek Salad 109
- Caramelized Cabbage With Pancetta & Apple 111
- Caramelized Roasted Vegetables 113
- Cumincrusted Oven Fries 116
- Lemony Green Bean Salad With Feta, Red Onion, And Marjoram 118
- Chicken With Kale, Red Onions, And Chili Salsa 120
- Tomato & Goat's Cheese Pizza 123
- Tofu With Cauliflower 125
- Cheesy Crockpot Chicken And Vegetables 128
- Hearty, Veggie Winter Soup 130
- Sweet Green Alkaline 132

Green Zinger Alkaline Juice 134

Sirtfood Chicken Salad 136

Turkey With Turmeric Sauce 138

Chinese Hot Pot Recipe 140

Lasagna Zucchini Cups

Ingredients:

- ½ lb. of beef (grounded)
- 8 cups of tomatoes (squashed)
- ¼ cup of parmesan cheese (grated)
- ½ cup of mozzarella cheese (shredded)
- 1 tablespoon of olive oil
- ½ teaspoons of oregano (dried)
- Kosher salt
- 3 medium zucchinis
- ½ onion (chopped)
- ½ cup of ricotta cheese
- Oil

- 2 cloves of garlic (diced)
- Parsley (chopped)
- Black pepper powder

Directions:
1. Preheat the oven to 350°F (175°C). Drizzle olive oil on a baking pan to prevent sticking.
2. Heat oil in a pan over medium heat. Add chopped onion and cook for 5 minutes, then add minced garlic and cook for 30 seconds.
3. Add ground beef, dried oregano, salt, and pepper to the pan. Cook until the beef is browned and no longer pink.
4. Strain out any excess fat from the pan and stir in the canned diced tomatoes. Reduce the heat to medium and let the mixture simmer for a few minutes.
5. Add ricotta cheese to the beef mixture and stir well. Turn off the heat.

6. Cut the zucchinis crosswise into thick slices. Using a spoon, scoop out the flesh from each slice to create wells for the filling.
7. Place the hollowedout zucchini slices on the prepared baking sheet.
8. Fill each zucchini slice with the beef and ricotta mixture, dividing it evenly among the slices.
9. Sprinkle grated Parmesan cheese and shredded mozzarella cheese over the filled zucchini slices.
10. Bake the zucchini cups in the preheated oven for 25 minutes, or until the cheese is melted and bubbly.
11. Remove from the oven and garnish with chopped parsley and additional grated Parmesan cheese, if desired.
12. Serve the Lasagna Zucchini Cups hot as a delicious and lowcarb alternative to traditional lasagna.

Beef Zucchini Enchiladas

Ingredients:

- 2 cloves of garlic (diced)
- Black pepper powder
- Kosher salt
- Cilantro (chopped)
- Oil
- 1 teaspoon of cumin seeds
- 1 cup of Monterey Jack cheese (shredded)
- 2 teaspoons of chili powder
- 1 lb. of beef (grounded)
- 1½ cups of enchilada sauce (red)
- 4 zucchinis (longitudinally sliced)
- 1 cup of cheddar cheese (shredded)

- 1 onion (chopped)
- Sour cream

Directions:

1. Preheat the oven to 350°F (175°C).
2. Place a pan over medium heat and add oil.
3. Once the oil is heated, add chopped onion and cook for 5 minutes. Then, add minced garlic and cook for another 1 minute.
4. Add ground beef to the pan and cook until the pink color disappears. Strain any excess fat.
5. Stir in 1 cup of enchilada sauce, cumin, chili powder, salt, and pepper. Reduce the heat to simmer for 5 minutes, allowing the flavors to meld together.
6. Cut the zucchinis into thin strips. Lay 3 strips on a chopping board, slightly overlapping them. Spoon a portion of the beef mixture onto one side of the zucchini strips and roll them up tightly. Repeat this process with the remaining zucchini strips and beef mixture.

7. Drizzle 1/2 cup of enchilada sauce over the rolled zucchini enchiladas. Sprinkle shredded cheese evenly over the top.
8. Grease a baking pan with oil and place the zucchini enchiladas in the pan. Bake in the preheated oven for 20 minutes, or until the cheese is melted and bubbly.
9. Garnish with chopped cilantro and serve hot. Optionally, serve with a dollop of sour cream.

Keto Zucchini Taco Shells

Ingredients:

- 3 cups of zucchini (grated)
- 1 egg (slightly beaten)
- ¼ teaspoons of garlic powder
- ¼ cup of almond flour
- ½ cup of cheddar cheese (shredded)
- Kosher salt
- Black pepper powder

For garnishing

- Bacon (cooked)
- Cheddar cheese (shredded)
- Salsa

- Cilantro (chopped)
- Avocado (sliced)

Directions:

1. Preheat the oven to 400°F (200°C). Place parchment paper on a baking pan to prevent sticking.
2. Keep the zucchini in a strainer and sprinkle some salt over it. Toss the zucchini and let it sit for 20 minutes. This step helps draw out excess moisture from the zucchini.
3. After 20 minutes, press the zucchini lightly to strain the moisture. Removing excess moisture is important to achieve a crispier texture.
4. In a bowl, combine the zucchini, almond flour, garlic powder, shredded cheese, egg, and pepper. Mix well until all the Ingredients: are evenly incorporated.
5. Scoop 1/4 portions of the mixture onto the prepared baking pan. Press the mixture down

and shape it into circular or oval shapes to resemble taco shells.
6. Bake the zucchini taco shells in the preheated oven for 25 minutes, or until they are golden and crispy.
7. Once the taco shells are baked, remove them from the oven and let them cool slightly.
8. Garnish the taco shells with your choice of toppings, such as fresh cilantro, crispy bacon, shredded cheddar cheese, diced avocado, and salsa.
9. Serve the Keto Zucchini Taco Shells as a lowcarb alternative to traditional taco shells. Fill them with your favorite taco fillings for a delicious and ketofriendly meal.

Chocolate Cherry Smoothie

Ingredients:

- 2 cups almond milk, unsweetened
- 3 teaspoons cacao powder
- 2 cups spinach
- 2 cups frozen cherries
- 1 teaspoon ground cinnamon

Directions:

1. Add all the Ingredients: to a blender and blend until smooth.
2. Pour into tall glasses and serve.

Antioxidant Wake Up Smoothie

Ingredients:

- 1 cup frozen cherries
- 1 ½ teaspoons green tea powder
- Stevia (optional)
- ½ cup blueberries
- 1 ½ cups vanilla almond milk

Directions:
1. Add all the Ingredients: to a blender and blend until smooth.
2. Pour into tall glasses and serve.

Crunchy Nut Coleslaw

Ingredients:

- 3 tablespoons peanuts, roasted
- 1 small radish, thinly sliced
- 1 medium carrot, grated
- 2 green onions, finely chopped (both the whites and greens)
- 5 tablespoons high fat yogurt
- 3.5 ounces white cabbage, finely shredded
- 2 ½ tablespoons sultanas
- 1 tablespoon low fat mayonnaise
- Pepper to taste
- 2 tablespoons fresh parsley, chopped to garnish

Directions:

1. Mix together mayonnaise, yogurt and pepper in a bowl.
2. Add rest of the Ingredients: into the bowl and mix until the vegetables are well coated.
3. Garnish with parsley and serve immediately.

Maple Syrup

Ingredients:

- ½ tbs guar gum
- 2 cups water
- 1 tbs maple flour
- 24 packets splenda

Directions:

1. Heat water and mentioned Ingredients: together. Now add take off the heat and add the guar gum to thicken the mixture. Cool and store in refrigerator. It has total of 24 grams of carbs.

Taco Salad

Ingredients:

- 2 tbs taco seasoning mix
- 4 oz cheddar
- 4 tbs salsa
- 4 cups lettuce
- 12 oz ground beef
- 2 tbs sour cream

Directions:

1. Heat the beef to brown and stir in the spices. Divide lettuce onto the two plates.
2. Top it with half ground beef mixture and sprinkle it witch salsa, sour cream and cheese. 2 servings contain 8 carbs.

Red Curry

Ingredients:

- 1 cup canned coconut milk
- ½ cup red pepper
- 1 tsp paprika
- 1 garlic clove
- 1 lb beef stew
- 1 tsp butter
- ½ tsp curry
- Cardamom, cinnamon and pepper

Directions:

1. Cook the meat and garlic in butter till they become brown and then add spices and fry for a few minutes.

2. Add coconut milk and red pepper, reduce heat and simmer it till fully cooked. It serves 3 with 5 carbs.

Hearty Avocado Salad

Ingredients:

- 99 g avocado
- 3 hardboiled egg
- 3 tbs olive oil
- 45 g brie cheese
- 35 g lettuce
- 14 green olives
- 45 g firm tofu
- Salt and pepper to taste
- 125 g plum tomatoes

Directions:

1. Heat 11 ½ of the oil in a small sauce pan.
2. Add the tofu and cook on both sides until golden brown.

3. Remove from heat and transfer to cutting board. Let cool.
4. Meanwhile, cube the avocado, brie, and hardboiled egg.
5. Add to a mediumsized bowl.
6. Finely chop the lettuce and cut the plum tomatoes in halves.
7. Add them to the bowl.
8. Cube the tofu and add the cubes to the bowl along with the green olives and remaining olive oil.
9. Mix to combine. Season with salt and pepper and decorate with parsley. Add in sliced jalapenos for a hot morning!

Spiced Tuna Salad

Ingredients:

- 5 Tbsp. mayo
- diced red bell pepper
- 5 thinly sliced scallions
- 1 chopped jalapeno rings
- ½ diced tomatoes, fire roasted
- 3 tsp. chili powder
- ½ tsp. ground cumin
- Juice from a lime
- 5 cans tuna

Directions:

1. To begin this recipe, you can bring out a mixing bowl and combine together the tuna,

tomatoes, jalapenos, scallions, and bell pepper.

2. Mix them together well using a fork, making sure to break up any of the big clumps of tuna.

3. Next, you can add the lime juice, cumin, and chili powder into the bowl, making sure to mix well before tasting to adjust the seasoning when necessary.

4. Using a rubber spatula you can slowly fold the mayo in with the salad so that it can become creamy.

5. Pile this salad onto a plate with some raw veggies.

Flax And Blueberry Vanilla Overnight Oats

Ingredients:

- Blueberries, almonds, blackberries, raw honey for topping
- ½ cup oats
- 1 cup water
- 1 cup lowfat yogurt
- 2 tbsp. flax seeds meal
- A pinch of salt
- ½ tsp. ground vanilla bean

Directions:

1. Add the Ingredients: to the bowl in the evening.
2. Refrigerate overnight.
3. In the morning, stir up the mixture.
4. It should be thick.

5   Add the toppings of your choice.

Savory Chowder

Ingredients:

- 2 pint half and half
- 2 chicken broth
- ½ kg. frozen cauliflower
- 1 red onion, chopped
- slices bacon bits, cooked
- 1 tsp. thyme
- 1/6 tsp. pepper
- 2 minced garlic clove
- 2 can clams with juice
- 1 tsp. salt

Directions:

1. To begin this recipe, take the cauliflower and follow the Directions:on the package to get it done right.
2. Drain out when you are done cooking and cube up the cauliflower if it is possible.
3. When that is done, bring out the crock pat and place all of the Ingredients: inside.
4. Cook on a low setting for about 66 ½ hours or until the onion has had enough time to soften.

Greek Yogurt With Mixed Berries, Honey, And Granola

Ingredients:

- 1 tbspn honey
- 2 tbspns granola
- 1 cup Greek yogurt
- 1/2 cup mixed berries i.e. strawberries, blueberries, and raspberries

Directions:

1. Place 1 cup of Greek yogurt in a bowl or serving plate
2. Wash and dry off the mixed berries. If you like, cut any larger berries in half.
3. Place a layer of Greek yogurt on top of the mixed berries.
4. Drizzle 1 tbspn of honey on top of the yogurt and berries.

5. To add crunch and texture, top with 2 tbspns of granola.
6. Gently whisk the Ingredients: into the mixture to incorporate them.
7. Eat the Greek yogurt, mixed berries, honey, and granola right now.

Salad With Mixed Greens, Tomatoes, Cucumbers, Olives, Feta Cheese, And Lemonolive Oil Dressing

Ingredients:

- 2 tbspns freshly squeezed
- 1 cup cucumber, diced lemon juice
- 1/2 cup Kalamata olives,
- 1 garlic clove, chopped pitted and halved
- 1 teaspn dried oregano
- 1/2 cup crumbled feta
- 8 cups mixed salad greens
- 3 tbspns extravirgin
- 2 cups cherry tomatoes, olive oil halved
- Salt and pepper to taste cheese

Directions:

1. Place the Klamath olives, cucumber, cherry tomatoes, feta cheese crumbles, and mixed salad greens in a large salad dish.
2. To make the dressing, combine the extra virgin olive oil, lemon juice, chopped garlic, dried oregano, salt, and pepper in a small bowl.
3. Add the dressing to the bowl of salad Ingredients:.
4. Make sure all of the salad's Ingredients: are welldressed by giving it a good stir.
5. Right away serve the salad and take a bite.

Grilled Salmon With Lemon And Dill, Served With Roasted Asparagus And Quinoa

Ingredients:

- 2 tbspn fresh dill, chopped
- Salt and pepper to taste

- 1 pound asparagus, trimmed
- 2 tbspns olive oil
- 1 cup quinoa
- 4 salmon fillets (avout 6 ounces each)
- 2 lemons, sliced
- 2 cups water or vegetable broth

Directions:
1. Turn the grill's heat up to mediumhigh.
2. On both sides, sprinkle fresh dill, salt, and pepper over the salmon fillets.
3. Arrange slices of lemon over the salmon fillets.
4. Lightly oil the grill grates to prevent sticking.
5. Grill the salmon fillets for 45 minutes per side, or until fully done and flaky. Depending on the fillets' thickness, the cooking time may change.

6. Set the oven to 425°F (220°C) and prepare the salmon while it is grilling.
7. Arrange the cleaned and trimmed asparagus on a baking pan and drizzle with olive oil. 10 to 12 minutes of roasting in the oven should yield tender results.
8. Heat the vegetable or water broth to boiling in a medium saucepan. When the quinoa is frothy and the liquid has been absorbed, simmer for about 15 minutes with the heat on low and the lid on.
9. Arrange the grilled salmon with quinoa, roasted asparagus, and lemon slices on the plate.

Hummus With Carrot Sticks

Ingredients:

- 3 tbspns lemon juice

- 2 tbspns extravirgin olive oil

- 1/2 teaspn ground cumin
- Salt to taste
- 2 cups canned chickpeas, drained and rinsed
- 1/4 cup tahini
- 2 cloves garlic, minced
- 4 mediumsized carrots, peeled and cut into sticks

Directions:
1. Put the chickpeas, tahini, garlic that has been minced, lemon juice, olive oil, cumin, and a dash of salt in a food processor or blender.
2. Blend the Ingredients: in a food processor until they are smooth and creamy, adding a tablespoon or two of water as necessary to achieve the desired consistency.
3. Give the hummus a taste and, if needed, add extra salt or lemon juice to tastetest the hummus.

4. Put the hummus in a bowl for serving.
5. Position the carrot sticks all around the hummus bowl.
6. Use the hummus as a dip or spread with carrot sticks.

Green Detox Elixir With Lemon And Ginger

Ingredients:

- Two cups spinach
- 2 cups kale
- 4 cups of liquid
- 2 lemons
- Of fresh ginger cut into 2inch pieces.
- An ice cube

Directions:
1. Thoroughly wash the kale, spinach, lemons, ginger, and spinach.
2. Lemons should be thinly sliced and kept aside.
3. Ginger should be peeled and sliced thin.
4. Lemon slices, ginger slices, spinach, kale, and water should all be put in a blender.

5. Blend at a high speed just until the mixture is well blended and smooth.
6. To get rid of any pulp or fiber, filter the elixir if required.
7. Move the potion into a pitcher.
8. For the flavors to meld, place the elixir in the refrigerator for at least an hour.
9. The Lemon and Ginger Green Detox Elixir should be served chilled over ice.
10. Enjoy a sip of this healthful and energizing green elixir!

Fat Burning Cocktail With Grapefruit And Orange

Ingredients:

- 1 cup Cold water
- 1 tablespoon of optional honey
- 1 medium grapefruit
- 2 oranges.
- An ice cube

Directions:

1. Juice the grapefruit and oranges first. Use a handheld juicer or a citrus juicer to cut them in half and squeeze the juice out.
2. Orange juice and freshly squeezed grapefruit juice should be combined in a blender.
3. Blend the contents in a blender along with the cold water until thoroughly blended.

4. For a hint of sweetness, you can add a tablespoon of honey to the blender. You can skip this step if you like a tangier flavor.
5. Pour the mixture into icefilled glasses once it has been thoroughly blended.
6. Use a spoon to gently stir the drink so that the flavors are dispersed throughout.
7. The Grapefruit and Orange FatBurning Cocktail should be served right away.

Smoothie Bowl

Ingredients:

- 1 tsp maple syrup

- ½ tbsp vanilla protein powder, vegan version if needed

- sliced kiwis, bananas and fresh berries

- 25g granola

- 1 tbsp mixed nuts and seeds

- 200g frozen mixed berries

- 1 ripe banana

- 75ml oat milk

- 1 tbsp almond butter

Directions:

1. Put the berries, banana, oat milk, maple syrup and protein powder in a powerful blender and blend until smooth.
2. Add a splash more milk if needed, but remember it needs to be quite thick.
3. Spoon the smoothie into a bowl and dot over the fresh fruit, granola and mixed nuts and seeds. Drizzle over the almond butter to serve.

Mushroom Baked Eggs With Squished Tomatoes

Ingredients:

- a few thyme leaves
- 2 tomatoes, halved
- 2 large eggs
- 2 large flat mushrooms (about 85g each), stalks removed and chopped
- rapeseed oil, for brushing
- ½ garlic clove, grated (optional)
- 2 handfuls rocket

Directions:

1. Heat oven to 200C/180C fan/gas 6. Brush the mushrooms with a little oil and the garlic (if using).
2. Place the mushrooms in two very lightly greased gratin dishes, bottomside up, and

season lightly with pepper. Top with the chopped stalks and thyme, cover with foil and bake for 20 mins.
3. Remove the foil, add the tomatoes to the dishes and break an egg carefully onto each of the mushrooms.
4. Season and add a little more thyme, if you like. Return to the oven for 10-12 mins or until the eggs are set but the yolks are still runny. Top with the rocket and eat straight from the dishes.

Apple & Sultana Porridge

Ingredients:

- 4 apples, cored and diced
- 100g sultana
- 100g porridge oat
- 500ml skimmed milk
- 1 tbsp brown sugar, to serve

Directions:

1. Put the oats and milk in a small pan and cook, stirring, for 3 mins until almost creamy.
2. Stir in the apples and sultanas, then cook for 2 mins more or until the porridge is thick and creamy and the apples just tender.
3. Ladle into bowls, sprinkle with sugar and eat immediately.

Cardamom & Peach Quinoa Porridge

Ingredients:

- 250ml unsweetened almond milk
- 2 ripe peaches, cut into slices
- 1 tsp maple syrup
- 75g quinoa
- 25g porridge oats
- 4 cardamom pods

Directions:
1. Put the quinoa, oats and cardamom pods in a small saucepan with 250ml water and 100ml of the almond milk. Bring to the boil, then simmer gently for 15 mins, stirring occasionally.
2. Pour in the remaining almond milk and cook for 5 mins more until creamy.

3. Remove the cardamom pods, spoon into bowls or jars, and top with the peaches and maple syrup.

Forest Fruit & Banana Smoothie

Ingredients:

- Frozen fruits of the forest
- Banana, sliced
- Lowfat fruits of the forest yogurt

Directions:

1. Whizz frozen fruits of the forest and sliced banana in a food processor with lowfat fruits of the forest yogurt.

Creamy Yogurt Porridge

Ingredients:

- 3 tbsp (25g) porridge oat

- 150g pot 0% fat robotic yogurt

Directions:

1. Tip 200ml water into a small nonstick pan and stir in porridge oats.
2. Cook over a low heat until bubbling and thickened. (To make in a microwave, use a deep container to prevent spillage as the mixture will rise up as it cooks, and cook for 3 mins on High.)
3. Stir in yogurt – or swirl in half and top with the rest. Serve plain or with one of our toppings (see 'goes well with').

Garlic & Bay Tilapia

Ingredients:

- A pinch of Old Bay Seasoning

- 1 tsp garlic salt

- 1 lemon, sliced

- 4*4oz fillets tilapia

- 1 tbsp butter

- 16oz mixed frozen broccoli & cauliflower

Directions:

1. Preheat the oven to 375F. Use low calories cooking spray to grease a 9*13 baking dish.
2. Place the butter and tilapia fillets in the baking dish. Sprinkle with old bay seasoning and garlic salt.
3. Next, place each tilapia fillet with a slice or lemon.

4. Fill the rest of the baking dish with the frozen cauliflower and broccoli. Dust the entire mixture with a pinch of salt and pepper.
5. Roast for 30 minutes, or until all vegetables are tender and the fish breaks upon slight pressure.

Strawberry & Banana Smoothie

Ingredients:

- ¾ cup rolled oats

- ½ tsp vanilla extract

- 2 tsp caster sugar

- 15 frozen strawberries

- 1 cup soy milk

- 1 banana, roughly chopped

Directions:

1. Add all Ingredients: to a food blender and process in pulses. Pulse until smooth. Separate into two serving glasses and serve immediately.

Garlic & Kale Soup

Ingredients:

- 4 cups raw kale, torn
- cups vegetable broth
- 2* 14oz canned garbanzo beans
- 4 plum tomatoes, chopped
- 1 tbsp Italian herb seasoning
- A pinch of salt & pepper
- 1 tbsp olive oil
- 10 garlic cloves, crushed
- 1 medium onion, chopped
- 1 cup fresh parsley, chopped

Directions:

1. In a large saucepan, warm 1 tbsp of olive oil over medium heat. Toss in the garlic and onion and cook for 57 minutes or until the vegetables have softened.
2. Throw in the kale and cook for 23 minutes or until the kale has completely wilted.
3. Add the remaining Ingredients:, except for the parsley and cook for 510 minutes.
4. Transfer the contents of the saucepan into a food process and process in pulses until smooth.
5. Transfer the saucepan contents back to the saucepan and simmer over low heat for 1520 minutes, or until the mixture has thickened.
6. Distribute the soup into servings and dress with parsley.

Red Wine Chicken

Ingredients:

- 1 tbsp paprika

- A pinch of salt and pepper

- 3 tsp olive oil

- 1 cup brown sugar

- 1 cup red wine lbs

- 3 chicken breasts, skinless, boneless, halved

- 3 tsp garlic, minced

Directions:

1. In a skillet warm 3 tsp olive oil over a high heat. Toss in the garlic and cook for 23 minutes or until the garlic has browned.
2. Add the chicken and fry for 1012 minutes on each side or until the chicken is cooked throughout.
3. Remove the oil from the skillet; drain it into a cup or container and set aside.

4. Dust the chicken breast with the brown sugar, paprika and garnish with red wine.
5. Cover the saucepan with a lid and leave to simmer for 20 minutes. Add a pinch of salt and pepper before serving.

Shish Kebab With Lemon Tahini Sauce

Ingredients:

- 1 bell pepper

- ½ tablespoon dried oregano

- ½ quartered red onion

- ¼ cup tahini

- 3 tablespoons divided lemon juice, divided

- 2 tablespoons divided olive oil

- 2 minced cloves garlic

- 2 small zucchini

- 1 pound cut to 1 inch pork loin

- ¼ cup water

Directions:

1. Mix 2 tablespoons of the lemon juice, the garlic, oregano, and a tablespoon of the oil in a bowl properly.
2. Put in the pork, mixing to coat. Alternately thread the zucchini, pork, onion, and bell pepper, on four 10inch spits.
3. Cover a grill pan or grill rack with cooking spray and heat up it to medium.
4. Grill them for about 8 minutes or until you see that the pork is well clear and the vegetables are soft enough for eating.
5. Meanwhile, mix the water, tahini, a tablespoon of lemon juice. And a tablespoon of oil in a small bowl until blended. Pour sauce and serve.

Barbecue Chicken Pizzas

Ingredients:

- 2 tablespoons gluten free barbecue sauce

- 2 thinly slices scallions
- 1/4 cup shredded reduced fat pepper Jack cheese
- 4 ounces cooked thinly sliced chicken breast
- 2 gluten free tortillas
- 2 tablespoons olive oil

Directions:

1. Preheat the oven to 200°C. Put the tortillas over the baking sheet. Brush every tortilla with tablespoon oil.
2. Top each one with a half of the cheese, barbecue sauce, onion, and chicken.
3. Bake for about 7 minutes or until the cheese on the topping is melted. Cut and serve.

Tomato Herb Marinated Flank Steak

Ingredients:

- 2 tablespoons chopped fresh marjoram
- 1 tablespoon chopped fresh rosemary
- 1 teaspoon salt
- 1/2 teaspoon freshly ground pepper
- 1 medium tomato, chopped
- 1 shallot, peeled and quartered
- 1/4 cup redwine vinegar
- 1 1/2 pounds flank steak, preferably grassfed, trimmed

Directions:

1. Puree tomato, shallot, vinegar, marjoram, rosemary, salt and pepper in a blender until smooth.

2. Set aside 1/2 cup, covered, in the refrigerator. Scrape the remaining puree into a large, sealable plastic bag.
3. Add steak and turn to coat. Refrigerate for 4 hours or up to 24 hours. Preheat grill to medium high.
4. Remove the steak from the marinade (discard the marinade). Oil the grill rack (see Tip).
5. Grill the steak 4 to 5 minutes per side for medium are or 6 to 7 minutes per side for medium, turning once and brushing the cooked side with some of the reserved sauce.
6. When the steak is cooked, turn it over again and brush with more sauce.
7. Transfer to a clean cutting board and let rest for 5 minutes. Thinly slice the steak crosswise and serve with any remaining sauce spooned on top.

Roasted Pork Tenderloin With Rhubarb BBQ Sauce

Ingredients:

- 1 small chopped onion
- 1 tablespoon cider vinegar
- 1/2 teaspoon divided freshly ground pepper
- ¼ cup ketchup
- ¼ cup packed light brown sugar
- 2 teaspoons Worcestershire sauce
- 2 tablespoons divided extra virgin olive oil
- 2 cloves minced garlic
- 2 cups sliced rhubarb
- 1 pound trimmed pork tenderloin
- ¼ teaspoon salt

Directions:

1. Preheat oven to 220°C. Heat up a tablespoon of oil in a saucepan by setting it to medium heat.
2. Add garlic and onion and cook, stir until it softens for about 2 minutes. Add ketchup, rhubarb, vinegar, brown sugar, Worcestershire sauce, and ¼ teaspoon of pepper; keep stirring until it blends together.
3. Make it simmer and keep stirring until the rhubarb and onions are soft for about 10 minutes. Turn the fire off and cover with lid.
4. Meanwhile, heat up another tablespoon of oil in an ovenproof skillet with medium high heat. Sprinkle the pork with pepper and salt; put it to the skillet and cook until fried on both sides for about 4 minutes. Put the skillet on the oven.
5. Cook the pork for about 12 up to 15 minutes. Move the pork to a cutting board and let it sit

there for at least 5 minutes to cool down a little. Slice, put sauce, and serve.

Seared Salmon With Sugar Snap Fennel Slaw

Ingredients:

- 1¼ pounds skinned wild Alaskan salmon
- 1 large fennel bulb
- ¼ cup lemon juice
- ½ teaspoon light brown sugar
- ½ teaspoon divided freshly ground pepper
- 3/4 teaspoon salt
- 3 tablespoons divided extra virgin olive oil
- 2 tablespoons minced shallot
- 2 cups trimmed sugar snap peas
- 2 teaspoons minced fresh chives

Directions:

1. Mix the lemon juice, shallot, 2½ tablespoons oil, brown sugar, ½ teaspoon of salt, and ¼ teaspoon of pepper in a bowl.
2. Put the 4 teaspoons of the dressing in bowl in a side. Slice the top of fennel bulb. Chop off 2 tablespoons of fronds and put it to a bowl.
3. Slice the bulbs in halve through the core and thinly. Slice the snap peas thinly into long matchsticks. Put in the fennel and peas with the dressing in the bowl.
4. Cut the salmon into 4 parts and put the remaining ¼ teaspoon of pepper and salt in it.
5. Heat up ½ tablespoon of oil in a nonstick skillet set in medium high heat.
6. Put in the salmon and cook for about 2 minutes. Turn it on the other side gently and continue to cook until it becomes dense in the center for about 2 up to 4 more minutes. Part the salmon and slaw into 4 plates.

7. Drizzle all of them with a teaspoon of the dressing and top with ½ teaspoon of fennel fronds and chives depending on your preference.

Mussels With Italian Turkey Sausage, Tomato & Basil

Ingredients:

- 1½cups chopped fresh plum tomatoes
- 1 large halved and sliced shallot
- 1 tablespoon extravirgin olive oil
- 1 cup dry white wine
- ¼teaspoon freshly ground pepper
- 4 pounds mussels
- 2 sweet turkey sausage or links hot
- 2 cloves minced garlic
- ¼cup chopped fresh basil

Directions:

1. Heat up oil in a pot in medium heat. Add garlic, sausage, and shallot and start cooking,

cutting up the sausage into little pieces for about 5 to 7 minutes until it is cooked.
2. Add wine, tomatoes, and pepper and make it boil by setting the heat on high. Stir in the mussels.
3. Cover with lid and cook for 4 to 6 minutes until the mussels are opened. Take off the heat and remove the unopened mussels if there are any.
4. Pour in the sauce from the pot and sprinkled with basil before serving.

Bang Cauliflower

Ingredients:

- 3 tablespoons of olive oil
- 1 tablespoon of Sriracha sauce
- Black pepper powder
- 1 tablespoon of cilantro (chopped)
- Kosher salt
- 2 tablespoons of sweet chili sauce
- 2 tablespoons of lime juice
- 3 cloves of garlic (diced)
- 1 large cauliflower

Directions:

1. Preheat the oven to 425°F (220°C).

2. Separate the cauliflower into florets, ensuring they are similar in size for even cooking.
3. In a bowl, combine the sweet chili sauce, Sriracha sauce, minced garlic, olive oil, and lime juice. Mix well to create the flavorful sauce.
4. Add the cauliflower florets to the bowl of sauce and toss until the florets are well coated and absorb the sauce.
5. Place the coated cauliflower florets on a baking sheet, ensuring they are evenly spaced. Season with salt and black pepper to taste.
6. Roast the cauliflower in the preheated oven for approximately 35 minutes, or until the florets are tender and caramelized, with crispy edges.
7. Once roasted, remove the cauliflower from the oven and transfer to a serving dish.

8. Garnish the Bang Cauliflower with fresh cilantro for added freshness and vibrant flavor.
9. Serve the cauliflower as a delicious and flavorful appetizer or side dish.

Butternut Squash Noodles

Ingredients:

- Kosher salt
- Parmesan cheese (grated)
- 16 oz of butternut squash noodles
- Black pepper powder
- 2 tablespoons of olive oil
- ¼ tablespoons of red chili flakes (crushed)

Directions:
1. Preheat the oven to 425°F (220°C).
2. In a large bowl, add the butternut squash noodles. These can be prepackaged spiralized noodles or homemade noodles made by spiralizing a butternut squash.
3. Drizzle oil over the noodles and season with black pepper, red chili flakes, and salt. Mix

well to evenly coat the noodles with the seasonings.
4. Transfer the seasoned butternut squash noodles to a baking sheet, spreading them out in a single layer.
5. Place the baking sheet with the noodles in the preheated oven and bake for approximately 10 minutes. The noodles should be tender and slightly golden.
6. Once cooked, remove the butternut squash noodles from the oven.
7. Garnish the noodles with freshly grated or shaved Parmesan cheese for added flavor and texture.
8. Serve the Butternut Squash Noodles as a side dish or base for other Ingredients: such as grilled chicken, sautéed vegetables, or a creamy sauce.

Burrito Butternut Squash Boats

Ingredients:

- 15 oz. of black beans
- 10 oz. of enchilada sauce
- 1 ½ cups of sweet corn
- 1 ½ cups of mozzarella cheese (shredded)
- Black pepper powder
- Olive oil
- 1 onion (chopped)
- 1 lb. of beef (grounded)
- 3 cloves of garlic (diced)
- ½ cup of cherry tomatoes
- Kosher salt
- 1 teaspoon of cumin powder
- Cilantro (chopped)

- 2 butternut squashes (sliced lengthwise)
- ½ teaspoons of chili powder

Directions:

1. Preheat the oven to 425°F (220°C).
2. Cut the butternut squashes longitudinally and brush the flesh with olive oil. Sprinkle it with salt and black pepper to season.
3. Place the seasoned butternut squashes on a baking sheet and bake for 2530 minutes, or until the flesh is tender and easily scooped out. Set aside.
4. Reduce the oven temperature to 350°F (180°C).
5. Heat oil in a pan over medium heat. Add the diced onion and cook for 5 minutes until softened, then add the minced garlic and cook for an additional 30 seconds until fragrant.
6. Add the ground beef to the pan and cook until browned, breaking it up with a spoon. Season

with salt, black pepper, chili powder, and cumin powder to taste.
7. Stir in the reserved butternut squash flesh, black beans, enchilada sauce, and corn kernels. Let the mixture simmer for a few minutes to allow the flavors to combine.
8. Fill the cavities of the roasted butternut squashes with the beef and vegetable mixture. Top each boat with shredded cheese and halved cherry tomatoes.
9. Place the filled butternut squash boats back in the oven and bake for an additional 1015 minutes, or until the cheese is melted and bubbly.
10. Remove from the oven and garnish with fresh cilantro.
11. Serve the Burrito Butternut Squash Boats as a delicious and satisfying meal.

Quinoa Salad From The Mediterranean

Ingredients:

- 1/4 red onion, chopped finely
- Pitted and sliced Kalamata olives, 1/4 cup
- 1/4 cup feta cheese crumbles
- chopped fresh parsley and mint
- cooked quinoa, 1 cup
- 1 cup halved cherry tomatoes diced cucumber half
- Olive oil and lemon dressing

Directions:
1. Cherry tomatoes, cucumber, red onion, Kalamata olives, crumbled feta cheese, parsley, and mint are all combined with cooked quinoa in a bowl.
2. Dress with a lemon olive oil mixture.

3. Gently blend by tossing.

Broccoli And Almond Salad With Alkalinity

Ingredients:

- Lemon juice, two tablespoons
- Extra virgin olive oil, 1 tablespoon
- Dijon mustard, 1 teaspoon
- 2 cups blanched broccoli florets
- 14 cup of almond slices
- 1 cup of raisins
- Pepper and salt as desired

Directions:
1. Broccoli florets, chopped almonds, and raisins should all be combined in a bowl.
2. Mix the lemon juice, olive oil, Dijon mustard, salt, and pepper in a another bowl.
3. Over the salad, drizzle the dressing, and toss just enough to mix.

Avocado And Cucumber Salad

Ingredients:

- 1/4 red onion, finely chopped
- 2 tablespoons fresh dill, chopped
- Juice of 1 lemon
- Drizzle of extra virgin olive oil
- 2 avocados, diced
- 1 cucumber, diced
- Salt and pepper to taste

Directions:
1. In a bowl, combine diced avocados, diced cucumber, red onion, and chopped dill.
2. Drizzle with lemon juice and olive oil.
3. Season with salt and pepper.
4. Toss gently to mix.

Stuffed Bell Peppers

Ingredients:

- 1 cup diced tomatoes
- 1/2 cup chopped spinach
- 1/4 cup chopped red onion
- 1/4 cup chopped fresh parsley
- 4 large bell peppers, tops removed and seeds removed
- 1 cup cooked quinoa
- Lemontahini sauce

Directions:
1. Preheat the oven to 375°F (190°C).
2. In a bowl, mix cooked quinoa, diced tomatoes, chopped spinach, red onion, and parsley.

3. Stuff each bell pepper with the quinoa mixture.
4. Place the stuffed peppers in a baking dish.
5. Drizzle with lemontahini sauce.
6. Bake for about 2530 minutes, until peppers are tender.

Zucchini Noodles With Pesto

Ingredients:

- 1/4 cup fresh parsley leaves
- 1/4 cup pine nuts
- 1/4 cup extravirgin olive oil
- 1 clove garlic
- Juice of 1 lemon
- 2 zucchinis, spiralized into noodles
- 1/4 cup fresh basil leaves
- Salt and pepper to taste

Directions:
1. In a blender or food processor, combine basil, parsley, pine nuts, garlic, and lemon juice.
2. Blend while gradually adding olive oil until you have a smooth pesto.

3. In a bowl, toss zucchini noodles with the pesto.
4. Season with salt and pepper.

Roasted Cauliflower Bowl

Ingredients:

- 1 teaspoon cumin
- 1/2 teaspoon paprika
- Salt and pepper to taste
- 1 cup cooked quinoa
- 1/4 cup chopped fresh parsley
- 1 small head cauliflower, florets separated
- 2 tablespoons olive oil
- 1 teaspoon turmeric
- Lemontahini dressing

Directions:

Preheat the oven to 400°F (200°C).

1. Toss cauliflower florets with olive oil, turmeric, cumin, paprika, salt, and pepper.

2. Spread cauliflower on a baking sheet and roast for 25-30 minutes.
3. In a bowl, mix roasted cauliflower with cooked quinoa and chopped parsley.

Mexican Tortilla Soup

Ingredients:

- 1 lime
- 1/2 bunch of coriander (cilantro)
- 2 large handfuls of spinach
- 2 cloves of garlic
- 1 chili / jalapeño (to your taste)
- 1 corn on the cob (about 4 inches long)
- Pinch of cayenne pepper
- 500ml of filtered water
- 2 teaspoons of vegetable bouillon or 1 yeastfree vegetable stock cube
- 1 sprouted tortilla wrap
- 1 ripe avocado

- 1/2 red capsicum (pepper)
- 1 tomato
- Pinch of black pepper and Himalayan (or the Celtic Sea) Salt

Directions:
1. Slice and toast the tortilla under a grill. Now prepare a vegetable broth by dissolving the stock in alkaline water and heating it.
2. Dice the bell pepper and tomato and roughly chop the coriander. Cut the avocado and then mince the garlic.
3. Add jalapeños to your liking and then chop your spinach.
4. Preparing the corn will be easy as you need to slice the kernels from the cob and then combine all of these vegetables into the broth. Head them all together then serve.

Lemon Chicken Stir Fry

Ingredients:

- 1lb boneless chicken breast, cut into pieces
- 10 oz mushrooms, halved and quartered
- 1 cup sliced carrots
- 2 cups snow peas (6 oz) stems and strings removed
- 1 bunch scallions, cut into pieces, white and green divided
- 1 tbsp chopped garlic
- 1 lemon
- ½ cup reduced sodium chicken broth
- 2 tsp corn starch
- 1 tbsp canola oil

Directions:

1. Juice lemon (3 tsp) and whisk with broth, soy sauce, and cornstarch in bowl. Separately grate lemon zest.
2. Heat oil in large skillet over mediumhigh heat. Add chicken and cook for 4 to 5 minutes. Place Chicken on plate.
3. Add carrots and mushroom to pan, and cook until carrots are tender. Add snow peas, scallion whites, garlic, and lemon zest. Cook for 30 seconds.
4. Add whisked broth mixture to pan, cook and stir until thickened. Add scallion greens and chicken. Cook 2 minutes. Place meal cooked meal on plate and enjoy.

Eggs With Ham, Cheddar And Chives

Ingredients:

- ½ tsp kosher salt

- ¼ ground pepper

- ¾ cup diced cooked ham

- ¾ cup shredded cheddar

- 1 tbsp unsalted butter

- 45 eggs

- 1 tbsp milk or water

- ¼ chopped chives

Directions:

1. Saulte ham in large nonstick skillet medium heat until brown.
2. Whisk eggs, milk, salt, and pepper in large bowl. Pour mixture into pan, cook and stir for

4 to 5 minutes. Adding cheddar and chives just before eggs are solid.

Veggie Smoothie

Ingredients:

- 1 small raw red onion
- ½ clove garlic
- 12 fresh dill or dried dill
- Dash sea salt
- 1 medium zucchini
- 1 medium tomato
- 1 stalk celery
- 1 ½ 2 cups of water (add hot water for soup)

Directions:

1. Blend 60 seconds or until smooth.

Blueberry, Flaxseed Yogurt

Ingredients:

- ½ cup Greek yogurt

- ¼ 1/3 cup blueberries

- ¼ cup flaxseed

Directions:

1. Mix Ingredients: and enjoy

Salmon Fillet With Citrus & Thyme

Ingredients:

- Kosher and salt

- 1 orange, sliced

- 1 lemon, sliced

- 3 lb piece skinless salmon fillet

- 1 tbsp olive oil

- 12 fresh thyme, chopped

Directions:

1. Heat oven to 375 F. Place the salmon on baking sheet. Drizzle with olive oil, and season with salt and pepper. Spread orange, lemon, and thyme around the fillet.
2. Roast salmon thoroughly, for around 2025 minutes.

3. Once place salmon on plate and spread orange, lemon, and thyme on top of fillet.

Kale, Edam Me And Tofu Curry

Ingredients:

- Two tomatoes, generally
- slashed Juice of 1 lime
- 7.05 ounce kale leaves tail eliminated and torn
- 0.5 ounce rapeseed oil
- Add one huge onion, chopped
- Add four cloves garlic, stripped and grated
- Add one enormous thumb (7cm) new ginger, stripped and ground
- Add one red stew, deseeded and daintily sliced
- Add 0.083 ounce ground turmeric
- 1/4 tsp cayenne pepper

- 0.166 ounce salt
- 8.8 ounce dried red lentils
- 1 liter bubbling water
- 1.76 ounce frozen soyaedamame beans
- 7.05 ounce firm tofu, hacked into cubes
- 0.166 ounce paprika
- 0.083 ounce ground cumin

Directions:

1. Put the oil over low medium hotness in a weighty lined stove.
2. Add the onion and cook for at least 5 minutes before inserting the garlic, ginger, and Chilli, then simmer for another 2 minutes.
3. Add the turmeric, cayenne, cumin, paprika, and salt. Eliminate and blend once more, prior to presenting the red lentils.

4. Pour in the bubbling water and cook for 10 minutes until the curry has a thick 'porridge' consistency, then, at that point, diminish the hotness and cook for another 2030 minutes.
5. Remove the soya beans, Tofu, and tomatoes and keep cooking for an additional 5 minutes. Add the juice of lime and kale leaves, then, at that point, stew until the kale is soft.
6. Place the buckwheat in a medium pot around 15 minutes until the curry is prepared, and add a great deal of bubbling water.
7. Take the water back to the limit and cook for 10 minutes (or to some degree longer assuming that you need gentler buckwheat. Void the buckwheat in a sifter and present with the dhal.

Salmon Sirt Super Saladsirt Food

Ingredients:

- Add 1.41 ounce celery, sliced
- Add 0.70 ounce red onion, cut
- Add 0.52 ounce pecans, cleaved
- Add 0.5 ounce capers
- Add one huge Medjool date, pitted and chopped
- 0.5 ounce extravirgin olive oil
- Juice ¼ lemon
- 0.35 ounce parsley, chopped
- 1.76 ounce rocket
- Add 1.76 ounce chicory leaves

- Add 3.52 ounce smoked salmon cuts (you can likewise utilize lentils, cooked chicken bosom or tinned tuna)

- Add 80g avocado, stripped, stoned and cut

- 0.35 ounce lovage or celery leaves, chopped

Directions:
1. Arrange the leaves of the serving of mixed greens on an enormous dish.
2. Blend every one of the leftover fixings and pour over the berries.

Turkey Skinny Stay Skewers

Ingredients:

- 0.166 ounce turmeric
- 1.5 ounce powdered nut butter
- 21.16 ounce | one 1/2lbs turkey bosom filets, cubed
- Extra water if needed
- Fresh coriander leaves
- 12 wooden sticks
- Two teaspoons minced garlic
- 0.5 ounce crunchy peanut butter (change in accordance with your tastes)
- 1 ounce earthy colored sugar, packed
- Salt to season

- 8 ounce light coconut milk

- Coconut oil splash

Directions:

1. 30 Minutes for dousing sticks. Segment turkey string onto sticks, then, at that point, set back.
2. In a different large, shallow dish, consolidate every one of the fixings together and race until blended.
3. Append sticks and marinade to a more profound preference for around an hour OR overnight.
4. Drain the turkey sticks while they are prepared to cook, holding the marinade.
5. Shower the oil splash on a nonstick dish/skillet and fry over medium hotness in two parcels (I did 6 for each bunch) until the underside is seared.
6. Move it to the opposite side and cook for another 45 minutes or until the turkey has cooked over.

7. Then again, prepare in a preheated broiler at medium high hotness under the barbecue/sear settings until cooked, turning once after around 10 minutes.
8. Switch the saved marinade to a little pot or pot and over high hotness convey to a bubble.
9. Diminish hotness to typical, and stew for 5 minutes while mixing or until the sauce is fragrant and thick. (Add additional water per cubicle

    provided that the sauce is too thick
10. Serve sticks with leaves of coriander, steamed rice or vegetables, and sprinkle with satay sauce.

Broiled Ginger Lime Chicken

Ingredients:

- 1 tablespoon lime zest
- 1 teaspoon ground cinnamon
- 1 teaspoon salt
- ½ teaspoon ground pepper
- ½ teaspoon freshly grated nutmeg
- ¼ cup finely chopped scallions
- 12 small bonein chicken thighs
- 2 tablespoons canola oil
- 2 tablespoons finely chopped fresh ginger
- 2 tablespoons lime juice
- ⅛ teaspoon cayenne pepper

Directions:

1. Line up a rimmed baking sheet or broiler pan with foil and cover it with cooking spray. Let the chicken dry.
2. Put on the set pan, skinned side up. Combine ginger, scallions, lime zest, oil, salt, cinnamon, pepper, cayenne, and nutmeg and season it on the chicken.
3. Put in a container and cover and refrigerate overnight. Set the broiler to high. Start broiling the chicken on the pan for at least 15 up to 25 minutes.

Sirtfood Bites

Ingredients:

- 250g dates
- 1 tbsp pure cocoa powder
- 1 tbsp turmeric
- 1 tbsp extra virgin olive oil
- 120g walnuts
- 30g dark chocolate (at least 85% cocoa content)
- Contents of a vanilla pod or vanilla flavor

Directions:
1. Put the walnuts in a food processor. Crush and add the chocolate. Now chop everything up until it is nice and fine.

2. Now add all the remaining Ingredients: and mix into an even dough. (possibly add a few tablespoons of water)
3. The dough now only has to be shaped into mouthsized pieces (approx. 15 to 20 pieces).
4. Put in an airtight container and chill. The bites can be kept in the refrigerator for up to a week.

Lima Bean Dip

Ingredients:

- Juice and zest of half a lemon
- 4 spring onions, cut into very fine strips
- Garlic clove, pressed
- 400g canned Lima beans, drained (alternatively canned white Greek beans)
- 3 tablespoons of extra virgin olive oil
- ¼ Thai chilli, cut into fine strips

Directions:

1. For the dip, simply process all the Ingredients: with the potato masher until the desired consistency is achieved.
2. Celery sticks and oat biscuits can be served with the dip.

Apple And Leek Salad

Ingredients:

- 1 tablespoon of cold pressed olive oil
- 1 tbsp rapeseed oil
- 125g sour cream
- ½ teaspoon turmeric
- ½ teaspoon curry powder
- 2 tbsp lemon juice
- Leaf parsley as desired
- ½ Stick of leek
- 2 apples
- 1 red onion
- 1 small bunch of chives

- Pepper

Directions:

1. First cut the washed leek into rings. The apple must be pitted and cut into wedges as desired. The onion must be diced.
2. Put the rapeseed oil in a pan and fry the onion until translucent. Briefly sauté the apple and leek.
3. In the meantime, mix the sour cream with the curry powder, olive oil, turmeric and lemon juice and season with pepper.
4. The chives must be cut into thin rings.
5. Mix the dressing with the Ingredients: from the pan and the chives and refine with the parsley to taste.

Caramelized Cabbage With Pancetta & Apple

Ingredients:

- 2 medium yellow onions
- 3 tbsp. Extra virgin olive oil, plus 1½ tbsp.
- 1 tbsp. Butter
- 1 tsp. Kosher salt
- 1 tsp. Hot pepper flakes
- 3 ounces thinly sliced pancetta, finely chopped
- 1 large green cabbage, cored and shredded
- 1 granny smith apple, peeled halved, cored and diced
- 1 tbsp. Lemon juice

Directions:

1. In a large skillet, heat 1½ Tbsp. of extra virgin olive oil. Add the pancetta and cook over moderate heat until crisp, about 8 minutes. Transfer the pancetta to a plate.
2. Using the same skillet, heat the remaining extra virgin olive oil and with butter. Add the pepper flakes, onions, cabbage and apple and sauté at medhigh, stirring constantly, until golden brown.
3. This can take anywhere from 2540 minutes, depending on how well your pot conducts heat. Keep scraping the caramel up from the bottom of the pot and incorporating it into the cabbage and onions.
4. When the mixture is soft and golden, add salt and taste to ensure it is well seasoned.
5. Keep browning until it reaches a caramel color – another 1525 Remove from heat and add the lemon juice.

Caramelized Roasted Vegetables

Ingredients:

- 2 yellow zucchini or summer squash, cut into ¾inchthick slices

- 1 eggplant, cubed, salted, allowed to drain for 30 minutes in a colander, and patted dry

- 1 head garlic, broken into unpeeled cloves

- 2 yellow onions, cut into 9 wedges each

- 1 fennel bulb, trimmed and sliced into wedges

- 1 or more red bell peppers, seeded and cut lengthwise into ½inchwide strips

- ½ cup   extra virgin olive oil

- Salt and freshly ground pepper to taste

- 1 sweet potato, peeled and cut into ½inchthick slices

- 1 unpeeled russet potato, cut into ½inchthick slices

- 2 green zucchini, cut into ¾inchthick slices

- 2 fresh rosemary sprigs, or 1 tablespoon dried rosemary

Directions:
1. Preheat the oven to 400 degrees F. Arrange all the vegetables in 3 or more large roasting pans, drizzle with the extra virgin olive oil, and sprinkle with salt and pepper.
2. Using your hands, toss the vegetables so that all of them are evenly coated.
3. Break up 1 of the rosemary spring and distribute it over the vegetables, or sprinkle the dried rosemary over them.
4. Roast until the vegetables are brown and tender, turning them once or twice to avoid sticking, about 1 hour.

5. Transfer to a large platter and serve warm, with a sprig of rosemary on top.

Cumincrusted Oven Fries

Ingredients:

- 2 tablespoons cumin seeds
- 1 teaspoon sea salt or to taste
- freshly ground black pepper to taste
- 1/2 cup homemade mayonnaise (optional)
- 2 1/4 lbs (1 kg) russet potatoes (4 medium)
- 1/4 cup   extra virgin olive oil
- 1 large nonstick jellyroll pan

Directions:

1. Preheat oven to 475ºF (246ºC). Scrub the potatoes but do not peel them. Cut lengthwise in 1/2" wedges.
2. Place the potato slices on the jellyroll pan. Drizzle with the   extra virgin olive oil and

sprinkle with the cumin seeds, salt and pepper.
3. Toss well then spread the slices in a single layer, cover tightly with aluminum foil and bake for 20 minutes until tender.
4. Remove aluminum foil, flip over each slice. Return tray to oven and continue baking uncovered for an additional 10 to 15 minutes, until goldenbrown.
5. Remove from oven and serve piping hot, with the mayonnaise on the side if desired.
6. Remove cauliflower from oven and place on serving platter. Top with bread crumbs and serve immediately.

Lemony Green Bean Salad With Feta, Red Onion, And Marjoram

Ingredients:

- 1/4 red onion, thinly sliced
- 34 sprigs fresh marjoram or oregano, leaves stripped and roughly chopped
- 1/4 cup   extra virgin olive oil
- 1 lemon, juiced and zested
- 1 pound green beans
- 4 ounces feta cheese
- dash agave nectar (or sugar to taste)

Directions:

1. Bring a pot of salted water to boil. Throw in green beans for about 4 minutes or until al dente. Drain and rinse in cold water.

2. Blend together lemon juice, zest, extra virgin olive oil and agave nectar. Combine beans and red onion, crumbled cheese, and marjoram. Toss with dressing. Chill until those lamp chops come off the grill.

Chicken With Kale, Red Onions, And Chili Salsa

Ingredients:

For the salsa:

- 1 tablespoon capers, finely chopped
- g parsley, finely chopped
- juice of a quarter of a lemon
- 130g tomatoes
- 1 Thai chili, finely chopped

For the rest:

- 1 tablespoon of olive oil
- 50g kale, chopped
- 20g red onions, sliced
- 150g chicken breast
- 2 teaspoons turmeric

- juice of a quarter of a lemon
- 1 teaspoon chopped ginger
- 50g buckwheat

Directions:

1. It is best to organize the salsa first: remove the stalk of the tomato, chop it finely and blend it well with the opposite Ingredients:.
2. Preheat the oven to 425 °. In the meantime, marinate the pigeon breast in some vegetable oil and a teaspoon of turmeric.
3. Heat an ovenproof pan on the stove and sauté the marinated chicken for one minute on all sides. Then bake In the oven for about 10 minutes, remove and canopy with aluminum foil.
4. In the meantime, briefly steam the kale. In a small saucepan, heat the red onions and ginger with vegetable oil until they become

translucent, then add the kale and warmth again.

5. Prepare buckwheat consistent with package Directions, serve with meat and vegetables.

Tomato & Goat's Cheese Pizza

Ingredients:

- 75g 3ozpassata or tomato paste
- 1 tomato, sliced
- 1 red onion, finely chopped
- 25g 1oz rocket arugula leaves, chopped
- 562 calories per serving
- 225g 8oz buckwheat flour
- 2 teaspoons dried yeast
- Pinch of salt
- 150mls 5fl oz slightly water
- 1 teaspoon olive oil
- For the Topping:
- 75g 3ozfeta cheese, crumbled

Directions:

1. In a bowl, combine all the Ingredients: for the pizza dough then allow it to face for a minimum of an hour until it's doubled in size. Roll the dough bent a size to suit you.
2. Spoon the cassata onto the bottom and add the remainder of the toppings. Bake In the oven at 200C/400F for 1520 minutes or until browned at the sides and crispy and serve.

Tofu With Cauliflower

Ingredients:

- Juice of a 1/4 lemon
- 200g tofu
- 200g cauliflower, roughly chopped
- 40g red onions, finely chopped
- 1 teaspoon finely chopped ginger
- 2 teaspoons turmeric
- 30g dried tomatoes, finely chopped
- 60g red pepper, seeded
- 1 Thai chili, cut in two halves, seeded
- 2 cloves of garlic
- 1 teaspoon of olive oil
- 1 pinch of cumin

- 1 pinch of coriander

- 20g parsley, chopped

Directions:

1. Preheat oven to 400 °. Slice the peppers and put them in an ovenproof dish with chili and garlic.
2. Pour some vegetable oil over it, add the dried herbs, and put it In the oven until the peppers are soft about 20 minutes).
3. Let it calm down, put the peppers alongside the juice In a blender and work it into a soft mass.
4. Cut the tofu in half and divide the halves into triangles. Place the tofu In a small casserole dish, cover with the paprika mixture, and place In the oven for about 20 minutes.
5. Chop the cauliflower until the pieces are smaller than a grain of rice.

6. Then, In a small saucepan, heat the garlic, onions, chili, and ginger with vegetable oil until they become transparent.
7. Add turmeric and cauliflower, mix well, and warmth again. Remove from heat and add parsley and tomatoes, mix well. Serve with the tofu In the sauce.

Cheesy Crockpot Chicken And Vegetables

Ingredients:

- ¼ cup water

- 4 boneless, skinless chicken breasts, cubed

- 1 cup chicken broth

- 1 cup milk

- 1 tablespoon parsley, chopped

- ¾ teaspoon. poultry seasoning

- 1 tablespoon AllPurpose flour

- 1 cup cheddar cheese, shredded

- 1/3 cup ham, diced

- 3 carrots, chopped

- 3 stalks celery, chopped

- 1 small yellow onion, diced 2 cups mushrooms, sliced
- 1 cup green beans, chopped
- ¼ cup Parmesan, shredded

Directions:
1. In a large bowl, combine ham, carrots, celery, onion, mushrooms, and green beans. Mix and transfer to your crockpot.
2. Layer the chicken on top, without mixing.
3. In the bowl, now empty, whisk broth, milk, parsley, poultry seasoning, and flour together until well combined.
4. Fold In the cheddar and Parmesan.
5. Pour the mixture over the chicken. Don't STIR.
6. Cover and cook on high 34 hours, or low 68 hours.

Hearty, Veggie Winter Soup

Ingredients:

- 2 fresh rosemary sprigs, leaves removed and chopped
- 1 cup of thinly sliced savoy cabbage
- cups of vegetable stock
- 1 15 oz canned of white beans, drained and rinsed
- Handful of parsley (flat leaf), chopped
- Leeks 3 Tbsp. coconut oil
- 3 leeks, green parts removed and thinly sliced
- 2 carrots
- 1 fennel bulb, thinly sliced
- 4 cloves of garlic, minced

- Sea salt (Celtic Grey, Himalayan, or Redmond Real Salt) and pepper

Directions:

1. In a large soup pot, heat the oil over mediumlow heat, add leeks, carrots, and fennel and cook until leeks are soft and slightly browned, about 58 minutes.
2. Add the garlic, rosemary and cook for another minute. Add the cabbage and sauté another minute.
3. Add stock and bring to a boil. Add the beans and cook on low for 10–15 minutes, until veggies are tender.
4. Stir in the parsley and season with salt and pepper to taste

Sweet Green Alkaline

Ingredients:

- 1 bunch swiss chard
- Handful fresh mint
- 1 cucumber
- 1 pear
- 1 tbsp of chia seeds (optional) mix in with juice to neutralize and slow down the metabolism of any sugars in the pear.

Directions:

1. Suggested juicing order swiss chard, pear, mint, cucumber – juice cucumber last to flush as much flavor as possible from juicer.
2. SWISS CHARD – roughly chop across the stem, then roll up the leaves to juice

3. PEAR – no need to peel. Add more or less depending on level of sweetness, for me 2 was perfect.
4. MINT – tightly ball up the leaves to juice, juicing the stems will add more mint flavor.

Green Zinger Alkaline Juice

Ingredients:

- 2 inch piece of Ginger

- Big handful of String Beans (amazing how much juice they kick up)

- 2 Pears

- 2 whole Cucumbers

- 1 Lemon

- 1 to 2 tbsp Chia Seeds (add after juice is made)

Directions:

1   Chia is comprised of 50% Omega 3 Fatty Acids, and is a very healthy fat that will slows down the metabolization of any sugars in the pears, avoiding any insulin spikes.

2   When you add Chia Seeds to a green drink, at first they will float to the top.

Sirtfood Chicken Salad

Ingredients:

- Medjool (1 date, finely chopped)
- Coriander (1 tsp, chopped)
- Turmeric (1 tsp, ground)
- Curry powder (1/2 tsp)
- Red onion (1/4 cup, diced)
- Bird's eye chili (1 pepper)
- Chicken breast (1/2 cup, cooked)
- Lemon (1/4 of a lemon juice)
- Walnut (6 halves, finely chopped)
- Greek yogurt (1/3 cup, skimmed)
- Arugula (1/3 cup, for serving)

Directions:

1. Chop the chicken into cubes. Cook the chicken pieces.
2. Mix the cilantro, Greek yogurt, lemon juice, and all the seasonings in a bowl.
3. Add all remaining ingredients then mix gently.
4. Arrange the thoroughly washed arugula on the serving plate. Put the mixture on them and it's ready.

Turkey With Turmeric Sauce

Ingredients:

- Red and yellow bell peppers (4 nos, in total)
- Powdered turmeric (2 tablespoons)
- Olive oil (1/2 cup)
- Turkey (breast or thigh, 750g)
- Salt, pepper to taste

Directions:
1. Chop the turkey into cubes.
2. Take 2 tablespoons of olive oil in a large bowl.
3. Add turmeric and mix well.
4. Add the turkey to the mixture and mix once more.
5. Cover the bowl and leave it in the refrigerator for 34 hours.
6. Clean the stems and seeds of the peppers, chop nely and set aside.

7. Put the meat in a large skillet and cook it on medium heat until it releases and absorbs its water.
8. Turn the heat down and cook until the meat is tender and add salt.
9. Take the remaining olive oil in another pan and sauté the peppers until they soften.
10. Transfer the turkey to a large serving plate and add the peppers to it.

Chinese Hot Pot Recipe

Ingredients:

- Anise (1 star) Broccoli (0.6 cup)

- Tomato puree (1 teaspoon)

- Parsley (2.6 tablespoons)

- Fresh coriander (2.6 tablespoons)

- Miso paste (1 tbsp)

- Lime (Juice, 1/2 lime)

- Broth (2 cups)

- Carrot (0.5 carrot)

- Prawns (0.7 cups, raw tiger)

- Mung bean sprout (0.6 cups)

- Noodles (0.3 cups, cooked)

- Chestnuts (0.3 cups, cooked)

- Tofu (0.7 cups, rm)
- Sushi ginger (0.2 cups, chopped)

Directions:
1. Start by bringing a large pot.
2. Chop tofu, sushi ginger, and carrot.
3. Crush the anise or use ground one.
4. Finely chop the coriander and parsley.
5. Put the parsley sprigs, puree, anise, coriander sprigs, chicken stock, and lemon juice in the saucepan.
6. Cook for 10 minutes.
7. Add all the Ingredients: except the sushi ginger and miso paste and cook until the prawns are cooked through.
8. Tip: Mix gently occasionally while cooking.
9. Remove from heat and stir in the sushi ginger and miso paste.

www.ingramcontent.com/pod-product-compliance
Lightning Source LLC
LaVergne TN
LVHW010224070526
838199LV00062B/4714